PEACE
by
PEACE

Your Part in Cultivating a Harmonious World

FESTIVAL OF THE FUTURE 5784

CREDITS

Produced by
Festival of the Future
*A division of The Moshiach Office
at Merkos 302*
ALL RIGHTS RESERVED

Rabbi Moshe Koltarsky
*Chairman, Merkos 302 and
The Moshiach Office*

Rabbi Mendy Kotlarsky
Executive Director, Merkos 302

Rabbi Shlomie Naparstek
Writer

Rabbi Levi Raskin
Rabbinical Advisor

Mrs. Pessi Stolik
Creative Direction & Editing

Mrs. Chana Cohen
(C Creative)
Graphic Design & Layout

Program dedicated by our friends at

Delmar Jewelers International
delmarintl.ca

ART BY MICHEL SCHWARTZ

And the world will be filled with the knowledge of G-d as the waters cover the seabed.

ART BY DANIEL WOLFE

WHAT IS MOSHIACH?

The Prophets in the Bible overflow with prophecies for a utopian world of peace and harmony for all humankind. Maimonides, at the end of his magnum opus, the Mishneh Torah, describes the era of Redemption in halachic detail: In that time to come, there will be no more wars, and food and luxuries will be as plentiful "as the dust of the earth". A Jewish king called Moshiach (literally: the anointed one), a descendant from King David, will rebuild the third Temple in Jerusalem and ingather the Jewish exiles to the Land of Israel from all over the world. Ultimately, all of humanity will share a common language of peace and recognize G-d, for He will be revealed in every aspect of the universe.

ART BY BARUCH NACHSHON

WHAT IS A FEAST OF MOSHIACH?

A highlight of Passover is the traditional 'Feast of Moshiach' held in its final hours. While most Jewish festivals commemorate an event from our nation's past, this evening is different. Tonight, we celebrate the future. We dedicate time to leaning into the message of our future Redemption by Moshiach (Messiah) and its relevance to us as we eagerly anticipate its arrival.

During the Feast of Moshiach, we traditionally partake in Matzah, drink four cups of wine, sing soulful melodies, and hear inspiring insights.

Matzah.

This famous Passover staple holds great spiritual significance, and in our tradition, it is referred to as the bread of faith, healing, and Redemption. We will talk a lot about redemption this evening; ingesting matzah is a literal direction to internalizing these lessons and making them personal.

While partaking of the matzah, meditate on its quality of sustaining hope in personal, as well as national, redemption.

4 Cups of Wine.

Our sages teach that the four cups align with the four unique expressions of redemption that are mentioned in the Torah at the time of our freedom from slavery in Egypt, but refer, more largely, to our complete redemption with Moshiach. Note that the intention while drinking the wine is most paramount of all meditations of the Moshiach feast.

While drinking the wine, think positively of the future. Recognize that among all the miracles that G-d has performed for our nation to save us from our enemies, the deliverance of our generation is ultimate and final.

Song.

Words can express what is
in our heart, but music is the
language of the soul. When
celebrating a future redemption,
we must reach beyond our
mundane trappings and
communicate with our souls.

*Listen in for the inner meaning
in each song, beyond the words.
Redemption begins from deep
within, and a \melody can open
up my soul to the process.*

Insights.

This is a special time to hear and share
Torah thoughts and life lessons. These
exchanges will help take the concept
of Moshiach from the abstract and
provide relevant lessons that can make a
change in your life here and now.

*Participating in this special feast of
Moshiach, the future Redemption is not
just an anticipated event, but relevant
and practical. How is this evening
moving me closer toward spirituality,
G-d and readiness to be redeemed?*

And a wolf shall lie with a lamb, and a leopard shall lie with a kid; and a calf and a lion cub and a fatling [shall lie] together, and a small child shall lead them. Isaiah 11:6

ART BY BARUCH NACHSHON

EVERLASTING PEACE

There will come a time when predatory animals will coexist in harmony with their former prey. This is also an allusion to a dynamic of drastic changes in human interaction, and in the fabric of society as a whole. Peace will reign between nations and cultures and amongst neighbors and friends, at home and in the streets.

Join us on a journey of redemption.

PART 2:
Dissolving Divisions

PART 1:
The Unspoken Narrative

The Unspoken Narrative

We have yet to achieve peace in practice, but have nonetheless adopted it as an axiomatic ideal.

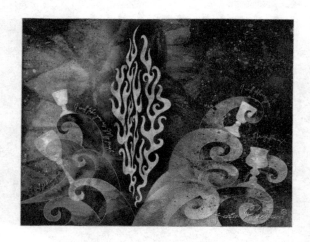

ART BY KARIN FOREMAN

The Rabbi & the Inmate

On the eve of Passover, Rabbi Meir Kaplan of Vancouver City rushed through his personal and communal holiday preparations and traveled out to a maximum-security prison to visit a Jewish inmate.

What the rabbi knew in theory became clearly evident to him at this meeting of Jewish souls on the eve of the Festival of our Freedom: G-d shines the light of redemption even—and especially— when circumstances seem darkest.

Swords to Plowshares

וְכִתְּתוּ חַרְבוֹתָם לְאִתִּים וַחֲנִיתוֹתֵיהֶם לְמַזְמֵרוֹת
לֹא יִשָּׂא גוֹי אֶל גּוֹי חֶרֶב וְלֹא יִלְמְדוּ עוֹד מִלְחָמָה.

*And they shall beat their swords into plowshares and their spears
into pruning hooks. Nation shall not take up sword against nation;
they shall never again know war.*

Isaiah 2:4

Even the worst people on the planet are ashamed to
be seen as the aggressor. We can see this as a sign that
society is moving closer to a time when all wars will end.

The Letter Vav (or Vov)

▶ I'M THE 6TH LETTER OF THE ALEF-BET.

▶ I'M A STRAIGHT VERTICAL LINE.

▶ MY NUMERICAL VALUE IS 6.

▶ I SOUND LIKE THE ENGLISH V (BUT I ALSO FUNCTION AS A VOWEL: / OO / OR / OŬ /)

To understand how the messianic promise of serenity and peace can be so close in a world that seems so chaotic, just peek into a Shabbat-observant Jewish home . The switch from the last-minute tumult of preparations to the serenity of Shabbat takes but one moment. And if we look just a bit beneath the surface, we can see it right now.

REFLECT

I orient myself to see global events as positive progress toward a more peaceful world. Even a century ago, acts of aggression were so pervasive, they barely registered as news events. I see the discomfiture with the global conflicts of today as proof of an unprecedented global consciousness for peace.

Cup 1

CELEBRATE

"L'CHAIM TO PEACE IN ISRAEL AND THE WHOLE WORLD. MAY WE MERIT TO SEE THE FULFILLMENT OF ISAIAH'S TWO-AND-A-HALF THOUSAND YEAR IDEAL OF A NEW WORLD ORDER. MAY HASHEM GRANT A SUSTAINED AND REAL END TO ALL SUFFERING, WAR AND BLOODSHED, WITH THE BLESSING OF MOSHIACH, TODAY!"

ART BY MICHEL SCHWARTZ

SING

הֲבֵאנוּ שָׁלוֹם עֲלֵיכֶם

הֲבֵאנוּ שָׁלוֹם עֲלֵיכֶם

הֲבֵאנוּ שָׁלוֹם עֲלֵיכֶם

הֲבֵאנוּ שָׁלוֹם, שָׁלוֹם, שָׁלוֹם עֲלֵיכֶם

Hevenu Shalom Aleichem

Hevenu Shalom Aleichem

Hevenu Shalom Aleichem

Hevenu Shalom, Shalom, Shalom Aleichem

We brought peace upon you.

With One Heart

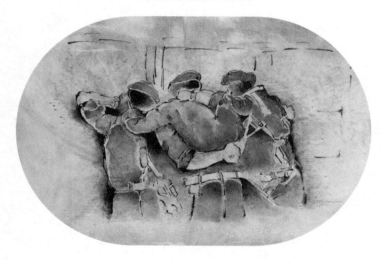

ART BY SHABSAI

Dissolving Divisions

Our enemies came to battle a nation, but at the gates, they found a family.

ART BY MICHEL SCHWARTZ

All Israel are One

Three months after October 7, 2023,
a young IDF soldier was released from
the hospital. He had lost his leg, and
many of his comrades lost their lives.
What makes it all worth it? He shares
his message with the world.

ART BY DAVORA LILIAN

The Soul of Everything

וְגָר זְאֵב עִם כֶּבֶשׂ . . .
כִּי מָלְאָה הָאָרֶץ דֵּעָה אֶת ה' . . .

And a wolf shall lie with a lamb . . .
for the land shall be full of knowledge of G-d…

Isaiah 11:6,9

When we reach deeper into ourselves to bring
out our inner core, our differences fade away.
We don't need a tragedy to make it happen;
we can make the conscious choice to live with
soul-centricity every day.

The Letter Shin

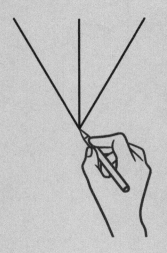

- ► I'M THE 21ST LETTER OF THE ALEF-BET.

- ► I START AT A POINT, AND THEN BLOOM UPWARD WITH 3 VERTICAL LINES IN 3 DIRECTIONS: RIGHT, LEFT & CENTER.

- ► MY NUMERICAL VALUE IS 300.

- ► I SOUND LIKE THE ENGLISH / SH /

All three lines, although they sprout in different directions, can coexist in this beautiful letter for they are all sourced in a single starting point.
Two Jews. Three Opinions. One G-dly core.

REFLECT

Two managers who are competitors on the work floor stand in unity in the CEO's office. Similarly, whatever my differences with a fellow Jew, they disappear when faced by our higher calling. I do not need to focus solely on similarities or areas of compromise. Instead, I take my cue from the messianic ideal and recognize that at the core we are all one.

Cup 2

CELEBRATE

"L'CHAIM! MAY WE LEARN FROM
ONE ANOTHER. MAY WE MERIT
THE DISSOLUTION OF EXTERNAL
BARRIERS BETWEEN PEOPLE AND
PURSUE PEACE. MAY HASHEM
SEE THE JEWISH PEOPLE'S
TREMENDOUS WIDESPREAD
UNITY AND HEAR OUR PRAYERS
TO BRING MOSHIACH SPEEDILY!"

ART BY MOULLY ART

SING

הִנֵּה מַה טּוֹב וּמַה נָּעִים שֶׁבֶת אָחִים גַּם יַחַד
הִנֵּה מַה טּוֹב וּמַה נָּעִים שֶׁבֶת אָחִים גַּם יַחַד
הִנֵּה מַה טּוֹב וּמַה נָּעִים —
שֶׁבֶת אָחִים, שֶׁבֶת אָחִים גַּם יַחַד

Hineh mah tov u-ma na'im shevet achim gam yachad.
Hineh mah tov u-ma na'im shevet achim gam yachad.
Hineh mah tov u-ma na'im —
shevet achim, shevet achim gam yachad.

Behold how good and how pleasant it is
for siblings to dwell together.

With One Heart

ART BY MIRA EISEN

Peace Upon the Home

Focus on a higher ideal together and peace will reign, forever.

ART BY LEON ZERNITSKY

The Miracle of Mimi

Issy and Mandy* got married,
but though they stuck it out over
two decades, they had a hard time
getting along. Then came what seemed
like their biggest challenge yet:
the miraculous Mimi.

*names changed for privacy

PAPERCUT BY MARCI WIESEL

דָּרֵישׁ רַבִּי עֲקִיבָא:
אִישׁ וְאִשָּׁה זָכוּ – שְׁכִינָה בֵּינֵיהֶן.

*Rabbi Akiva taught: If a man and woman merit reward through
a faithful marriage, the Divine Presence rests between them.*

Talmud Sotah 17a

What is the key to a peaceful home?
Spending quality time as a couple?
Honing communication skills? Buying gifts?
These are all good things, but not the secret sauce
to the most tranquil relationship, which comes
from focusing on a mutual spiritual mission.

The Letter Lamed

▶ I'M THE 12TH LETTER OF THE ALEF-BET.

▶ I HAVE A HORIZONTAL BODY WITH A LINE PROTRUDING UPWARD FROM ITS LEFT EDGE AND A LINE PROTRUDING DOWNWARD FROM ITS RIGHT EDGE.

▶ MY NUMERICAL VALUE IS 30.

▶ I SOUND LIKE THE ENGLISH L.

When two lameds, each extending itself in reaching for G-d (a yod), face each other in mutual acknowledgment, they form the outline of one whole heart.

REFLECT

In seeking a beautiful relationship with my spouse and my family, I adopt a Moshiach-style peace. I seek the spirituality and G-dliness that we can introduce into our lives, to make the relationship deep and enduring.

Cup 3

CELEBRATE

"L'CHAIM! MAY HASHEM BLESS
OUR FAMILIES WITH HEALTH AND
HAPPINESS AND MAY WE SEE
NACHAT FROM OUR CHILDREN.
MAY WE LEARN AND GROW IN
OUR JUDAISM AND FOCUS ON THE
SOURCE OF ALL THE GOOD THINGS
IN LIFE. HASHEM, BLESS US
WITH SHALOM BAYIT, PEACE IN
THE HOME, MAKING OUR HOMES
READY TO INVITE MOSHIACH
IMMEDIATELY!"

ART BY RIVKY DAVID

עוֹד יִשָּׁמַע בְּעָרֵי יְהוּדָה וּבְחֻצוֹת יְרוּשָׁלַיִם
קוֹל שָׂשׂוֹן וְקוֹל שִׂמְחָה קוֹל חָתָן וְקוֹל כַּלָּה

Od yishama b'arei Yehudah uv'chutzot Yerushalayim.
Kol sasson v'kol simcha, kol chattan v'kol kallah.

Yet again there shall be heard... in the cities of Judah,
and in the streets of Jerusalem,
the voice of joy and the voice of gladness,
the voice of the bridegroom and the voice of the bride.

ART BY MICHOEL MUCHNIK

Completing the Puzzle

We can achieve a world of harmony:
Peace by peace and piece by piece.

ART BY BARUCH NACHSHON

Elevated Effort

When the Master places
before you an insurmountable
challenge, you can try to
comprehend how to complete
the job, and give up because it is
impossible. Or you can just keep
putting your best foot forward
and trust in the mission.

PAPERCUT BY ELENA KALMAN

Transformed for Good

עָשָׂה מִצְוָה אַחַת הֲרֵי הִכְרִיעַ אֶת עַצְמוֹ
וְאֶת כָּל הָעוֹלָם כֻּלּוֹ לְכַף זְכוּת
וְגָרַם לוֹ וְלָהֶם תְּשׁוּעָה וְהַצָּלָה

*If one performs even one deed, they he can tip themselves himself
and the whole world to the side of merit bringing to themselves, and
to all, himself and them redemption and salvation.*

Rambam, Hil. Teshuva 3:4

World peace can be achieved peace by peace:
one person, one home and one community at a time.

The Letter Closed Mem

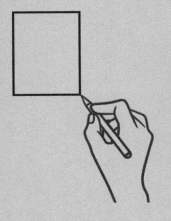

▶ מ IS THE 13TH LETTER OF THE ALEF-BET; I AM ITS DERIVATIVE, THE 24TH (ONE OF FIVE UNIQUE LETTERS THAT CHANGE SHAPE AT THE ENDING OF A WORD).

▶ I AM A BOX, COMPLETELY CLOSED ON ALL SIDES.

▶ THE NUMERICAL VALUE OF מ IS 40, MINE IS 600.

▶ I SOUND LIKE THE ENGLISH M.

The framework of G-d's creation of the world includes a space for human effort to contribute to its final perfection. Each positive action brings us closer and closer to filling in the gap to form a structure of eternal peace.

REFLECT

The world is becoming more Moshiach-like. I must train myself to be more conscious of the fact that we are nearing global perfection. When I establish a sphere of peace in my immediate circle, the effects can reverbert to the other end of the world. My next action can be the last piece towards achieving peace.

Cup 4

CELEBRATE

"L'CHAIM! MAY HASHEM GRANT US
THE RECOGNITION OF LIVING
MOSHIACH-ORIENTED LIVES TODAY
AT THE CUSP OF WORLD REDEMPTION.
MAY HE EMPOWER US IN THE PURSUIT OF
PEACE IN OUR OWN LIVES AND EXTEND OUR
INFLUENCE ON THOSE AROUND US TO SET
A PRECEDENT AND A CHAIN REACTION SO
THAT FINALLY, THE ENTIRE WORLD WILL
ACHIEVE TRUE SHALOM—PEACE, WITH THE
ARRIVAL OF MOSHIACH, MAY IT HAPPEN
RIGHT AWAY!"

ART BY B. KIMMELMAN

SING

עוֹשֶׂה שָׁלוֹם בִּמְרוֹמָיו הוּא יַעֲשֶׂה שָׁלוֹם עָלֵינוּ
וְעַל כָּל יִשְׂרָאֵל וְאִמְרוּ, אִמְרוּ אָמֵן
יַעֲשֶׂה שָׁלוֹם
יַעֲשֶׂה שָׁלוֹם
שָׁלוֹם עָלֵינוּ וְעַל כָּל יִשְׂרָאֵל

Oseh shalom bimromav hu ya'aseh shalom aleinu
V'al kol Yisrael v'imru, imru amen.
Ya'aseh shalom
Ya'aseh shalom
Shalom aleinu v'al kol Yisrael

May the One Who creates peace on high bring
peace to us and to all Israel. And we say: Amen.

This is PEACE.

Make the last act yours.　　　　<　　　*Visualize* the underlying reality.

Lean on something higher.   *See* the core in everything.

ART BY MICHOEL MUCHNIK

Take it Home

Unite your inspiration with action. Commit to something small and experience enormous impact!

There is so much more on the topic of Moshiach and redemption that can inform and uplift you. Dedicate some time each week to further your knowledge of Moshiach and its centrality to a more meaningful life. Ask the rabbi to help guide your discovery.

SUITE|302